REFLECTIONS of YESTERDAY

The publishers are indebted to the photographers of the past, known and unknown without whose work this book would never have happened.

Thanks are also due to Reigate Corporation and the many local residents and business people who have provided the information essential to the production of this book.

Original material and research:
Dr. Alan Ingram

Photography:
Malcolm Pendrill, FIIP FRPS

Text:
Malcolm Pendrill in collaboration with John Ferguson

Design and Layout:
John Ferguson, ARCA FRSA

ISBN 0 9508230 0 7

First published 1982

Photoset and printed by Gavin Martin Ltd,
26-34 Rothschild Street, London SE27 0HQ

REFLECTIONS
of
YESTERDAY

A retrospective look
at Reigate and Redhill

by Alan Ingram & Malcolm Pendrill

Mace Bearers: 1911 & 1982.

Introduction

Within these pages you will discover Reigate and Redhill as they were between 1880 and 1925. The towns our parents and grandparents lived in.

For those old enough, this book will arouse many memories. Redhill Market on Saturday night, the Town Brass Band, boating on Earlswood Lake. The evenings at the Cinema Royal and the Picture Pavilion. Sherbet dabs, liquorice bootlaces and penny snowfruits and the illicit tuppenny packet of Woodbines "bought for dad".

Some of these photographs reflect life before the names of Mons and Passchendaele made grown men tremble and women weep. A time when a child dying of diphtheria was commonplace and a working man's weekly wage was counted in shillings.

This was the age that witnessed the first aeroplane flight, saw the development of the motor car and the beginnings of wireless. This book is more than a collection of evocative photographs. It is a tangible statement of the changes that have taken place during the last 100 years.

The source of material is mostly the commercial picture postcard, which sold for a penny or two. These cards are now revealing a wealth of information about life in Reigate and Redhill and hopefully, will stimulate a deeper appreciation of that which remains after a century of change and development.

This is not a book to hurry through. Rather the reader should linger over the pages, look at the faces of the children and ponder their future. The soldier going to war, the farmer in his field, the baker by his cart; for them this was their present time. For us, they are Reflections of Yesterday.

The top photograph shows Station Road Redhill as it is today, looking towards the Market Square.

Below is Bell Street Reigate, with the trees on the Castle Mound against the sky-line.

Redhill was created around the railway station which was built on its present site in the early 1840s, when the Ashford, Reading and Brighton lines were completed.

The Railway Company laid out Station Road and the road eastwards to the top of Redstone Hill. By 1860 a small settlement called Warwick Town was established. Redhill grew rapidly throughout the latter part of the 19th century, thriving as a centre of commerce because of the railway.

Reigate is first recorded in the 12th century when it was an area of small, scattered settlements. It was given to William de Warenne, on his installation as Earl of Surrey, and this family played a major part in Reigate's early development.

Until the end of the 18th century, the road system of the town centred on the old market place then standing at the junction of Upper West Street, Nutley Lane and Slipshoe Street.

The population in 1801, the year of the first census, stood at just over 2000 for Reigate and the surrounding area.

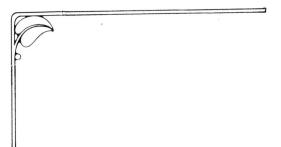

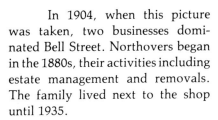

In 1904, when this picture was taken, two businesses dominated Bell Street. Northovers began in the 1880s, their activities including estate management and removals. The family lived next to the shop until 1935.

J. Knight & Son, drapers, have occupied their premises since 1883, when half the present site was used. In 1911 they acquired the Bunch of Grapes Inn next door, and extended their business. They also had a furniture store opposite the Priory.

Another photograph taken about 1904. Nearly eighty years separate this from its small counterpart, yet the buildings in this part of Reigate High Street remain almost unchanged. Now, shop facias are more prominent, the flower-filled window boxes no longer delight the eye and the Congregational Church has gone. In this old photograph a milk float can be seen outside Webb's Milk Shop.

Redhill High Street in 1904, looking towards the Square. Many of the popular shops of the day can be seen. Jones the Drapers and Jennings, who moved there in 1881, and are trading in the High Street to this day. A feature to note is the array of magnificent gas lanterns hanging from the shop facias.

Another animated street scene also photographed in 1904, showing Station Road Redhill, looking towards St. Matthew's Church. The spire can just be seen behind the trees. Many people will still remember the well-known clock above Tanner's the jewellers which, for decades, told the passing of time in Station Road.

The Post Office in Bell Street, Reigate, was built in 1895 and had a staff of 46 when this photograph was taken in 1909. Mr. G. Denyer was the Assistant Superintendent. He could look forward to earning a maximum of £180 per year. A town postman's wages were between 17 and 25 shillings a week; a messenger boy's, 6 shillings.

There were three deliveries a day. Postmen who used bicycles were paid an extra shilling a week to keep them clean, and those who rode were paid five shillings for horse keeping.

Good conduct stripes were awarded to the staff. One stripe for every five years of unblemished service. These were rewarded with a shilling a week for each stripe. Mr. Frost, a postman, had five stripes early in 1909. This award scheme was abolished in 1914.

The Post Office in the days of the "3d Purple-on-Yellow".

The facade of the buildings on the south side of Station Road, Redhill, from the Square to the Station, has changed little since it was built by the London and Brighton Railway Company in the 19th century.

This photograph taken about 1906 shows businesses with such evocative names as Surrey Tobacco Depot, the Redhill School of Music. Bon Marche and Hammond & Dawson.

The Cinema Royal was built where the Arcade now stands, and was advertising films with titles like "Let No Man Escape" and "Caught with the Goods" in 1914.

Nearer the Station on the south side, on waste ground by the railway, the Odeon Cinema was built in the late 1930s.

Station Road, Redhill at the time of the Boer War.

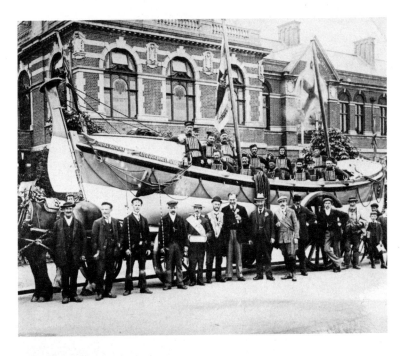

The photograph top left shows a Lifeboat Parade in 1907. The boat was drawn by a team of six horses around Reigate and Redhill to raise funds for The Royal National Lifeboat Institute.

The picture, top right, records a Civic Occasion. The commemorative service for the late King Edward VII, held at St. Mary's Parish Church on 20th May 1910. The Mayor leaving the church is Thomas Gregory.

Lower left: A photograph taken in Bell Street Reigate in 1905, which captures the peaceful atmosphere of a country town before the onslaught of modern-day road traffic.

Lower right: The Flying Scud public house in 1906. Owned by the Reigate Brewery, the pub was licensed until 1933 to sell only beer. The building has been used as a pub since 1867.

June 21st 1911, was a day these Reigate children wearing their
Sunday clothes despite the rain, would never forget. They are watching an
open-air entertainment, some smaller ones sitting on the shoulders of their older companions
in order to get a better view. All their lives they would remember
the Coronation of King George V.

In 1905, Kennetts of 25 Station Road, Redhill, advertised that they stocked the best assortment of Arms china in the neighbourhood. Frith's picture postcards, leather goods, brushes and combs could also be purchased. The sign on the right, for the premises next door, advises patients that the dentist attends on Thursdays.

Yesterday's stock-in-trade — today's collector's items.

A busy scene in Brighton Road Redhill, viewed looking towards the Reading Arch, a brick-built railway arch carrying the Reading branch line from Redhill station. This photograph, taken before the arch was widened in 1901, shows the studios of E. Dann & Son, Photographers.

Looking towards Redhill station from the Market Place. Nicol and Sons, well-known family drapers and ladies outfitters occupied the corner premises. In 1901, ten years before this photograph was taken, a serious fire occurred here in which two employees perished.

A fine view could be seen from the top of Reigate Hill in the early days of the century. Today it is screened by trees. The novelist Fanny Burney compared the view from Reigate Hill to that from the Malvern Hills when she passed through Reigate in 1779.

In this photograph Wray Lane can be seen and the bridle way which joins it at the bottom of the hill.

On the 4th May 1910, the Drinking Fountain on Colley Hill was opened. It was presented to the Corporation of the Borough of Reigate by Lt.-Col. Robert William Ingles, V.D., "for the Benefit of the Public". Sadly today it has fallen into disuse and has been much damaged.

The original Turnpike Road north, from Reigate, followed the route on the right of this photograph across what is now a car park. In 1824, this bend was shortened by making a cutting through one side of the hill. The two cars are a Daimler, with a Burton-on-Trent registration preceded by a 1907 Hotchkiss registered in London, with a Roi-Des-Belges body.

In 1825 the cutting was spanned by an iron suspension bridge designed by William Constable, the surveyor to the project. This bridge lasted for 85 years until it became unsafe, and was replaced by the present concrete structure in 1910. This photograph of a family outing was taken at Christmas time, shortly after the new bridge was opened.

June 20th 1906, a Gala Day, with bunting, when the New Public Swimming Baths were opened opposite the Municipal Buildings in Castlefield Road. The Buildings were erected through the generosity of Mr. J. B. Crosfield, a local resident.

The Opening of the Swimming Baths, 1906.

The Boating Lake on Earlswood Common in 1923. It was originally the site of clay excavations for a nearby brickworks.

After the 1914-18 War, the unemployed were given work clearing and excavating. The spoil was built up and formed the island which is in the centre of the lake.

It has been a boating lake since the 1920s, when skiffs, punts and a small steamer crowded the water. A number of businesses have rented the boating concession from the Borough Council.

The lower lake, called New Pond, existed as early as the 14th century and is stocked with fish. It was once popular for swimming and there was a diving board on the east side.

During the 1939-45 War, Canadian troops used the lake to practise driving vehicles through water.

Boating on the lake — Earlswood Common in the Twenties.

The census of 1901 showed that no more than 12 per cent of the country's population were earning their living from the land. This was due to the repeal of the Corn Laws. Since 1870 the national acreage of corn had shrunk by 30 per cent.

When war came in 1914 Britain was importing as much as 75 per cent of its bread grain.

Mechanical reapers and hay mowing machines like these in use at harvest time in Clifton's Lane, Reigate about 1906, were introduced in the late Victorian era. They were still horse-drawn well after the turn of the century. Hand reapers were paid 7 shillings and 6 pence an acre reaped.

At about this time William Willet formed his Daylight Saving Society, suggesting that clocks should be put back one hour in the Spring.

This delightful photograph was taken about 1908. The original was incorrectly titled as Sandcross Lane, but research has placed this landscape as Littleton Lane, which runs off Park Lane westwards and is now farmland.

Without any information about this photograph the imagination is free to create many interpretations as to the occasion. By the amount of foliage it is early spring and the shadows show that it is afternoon. Who are the two ladies? They appear to be about the same age. Could they be sisters or just friends?

It is doubtful if they have walked far. Perhaps they are visiting locally and have a carriage nearby for there are tracks in the lane. Outside the cottages stand two gentlemen in bowler hats who seem to be posing for the camera. Perhaps they all have a rendezvous. Altogether a delightfully enigmatic photograph.

A Surrey landscape in Edwardian days.

In 1627 William Ridley and others were fined for erecting cottages on Earlswood Common. An act of 1589 forbade the building of a cottage on less than 4 acres and the taking of lodgers. It was feared that overcrowding would increase the number of paupers to be supported by the Parish.

In 1909 the Reigate Stock, Share & Estates Co. Ltd. bought the "Roundabout" as the cottages were called. Proving too costly to modernise, they were demolished in 1960. This picture was taken in 1913.

Somerset Road, Meadvale in 1905, seen by the camera of Francis Frith. This village was the home of artist and engraver Samuel Palmer who lived and died here in 1881. He is buried in St. Mary's Parish Church cemetery.

The baker's van in this picture belonged to Keasleys, well known local wholesalers and bakers, renowned for their gingerbread, biscuits and boiled sweets. The business was established in 1726 and enjoyed Royal patronage.

In 1862 Redhill Common was the proposed site for a Military Prison. It was to cover 16 acres and the corner pillars which mark the area can still be seen.

The view across the Weald to the South Downs is now obscured by trees, but in 1915 when this photograph was taken, this aspect was open to the fine spire of St. John's Church. The Church was built in 1843 and rebuilt in 1889. The spire is the work of John Pearson, the architect of Truro Cathedral.

The dew pond on the lower slopes of Redhill Common was a popular rendezvous for boys of the neighbourhood who used it for sailing model boats, and in season, catching tadpoles in jam jars which they proudly carried home.

The pond was concreted in the 1930s but otherwise has changed little since 1907 when this photograph was taken.

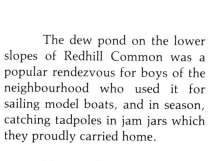

White Post Hill, Redhill in 1906. A private carriage and pair is drawn up by the Hospital and a mother is wheeling her baby in a wickerwork perambulator. The white house at the top of the hill was the first Post Office in Redhill. A sub-office to Reigate, it was run by John Comber who was also a builder.

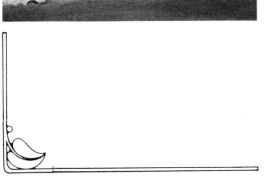

The Cottage Hospital, as it was known until 1907, was then renamed the Reigate and Redhill Hospital. It was built, with the entrance facing Redhill Common, in 1871. There had, in fact, been an earlier hospital in Albert Road North, in Reigate. In 1923 the establishment was again renamed as the East Surrey Hospital.

Shaw's Corner was originally the site of a workhouse. It got its name from Simeon Shaw who, in the 19th century, had a blacksmith's shop there. Later, at the turn of the century it was one of the proposed sites for the new Municipal Buildings. This proposal created much controversy but finally Castlefield Road, Reigate was chosen. The buildings were erected there in 1901.

In 1924 the fine chestnut tree was removed from the island in the centre of Shaw's Corner to make room for a memorial to the fallen of the 1914-18 war.

This 1904 photograph shows St. Paul's Church when it was only two years old. The drinking fountain which also stood on the island can be seen in the picture. This was eventually moved to its present site on Redhill Common opposite the Hospital. It was dedicated to the memory of a Mr. Gedge, who died in Zermatt, Switzerland in 1897.

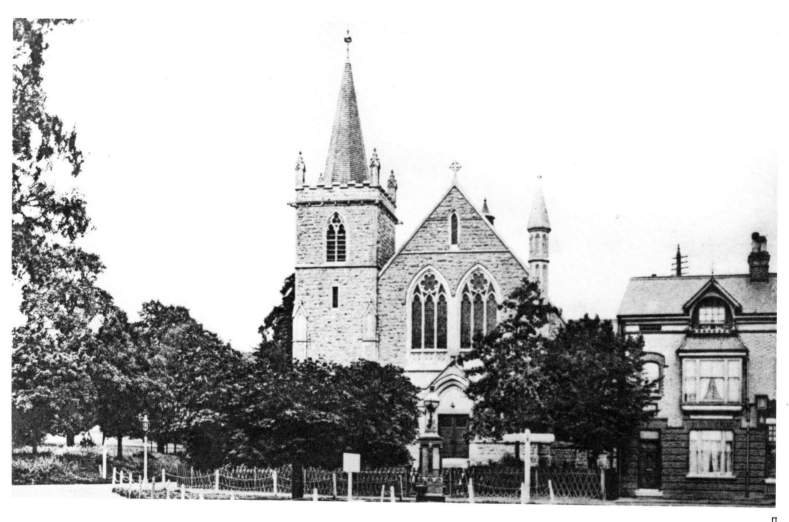

St. Paul's Church, Shaw's Corner, in 1904, the year in which Mr. Edward Elgar was knighted.

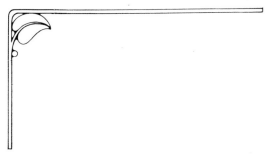

"Soon after midday on September 9th 1914, the first bodies of troops entered Reigate and then onwards during the afternoon they were followed up by the remaining detachments of the body which made up the column." So quoted the Surrey Mirror of Friday September 11th 1914.

Many thousands of Territorials marched from Aldershot to Dover for embarkation to France and the Western Front. A few weeks before, they had been clerks, postmen, shopkeepers etc. Now, plenty of fresh air and hard work on the Surrey heathland had given them the appearance of healthy, sunburnt troops.

As each Company, Battery or Troop passed through the densely packed streets they were greeted with cheers of pride by the residents. Reigate High Street rang to the strains of "Tipperary", and other patriotic songs.

On the outskirts of the town each unit was met by a Scout, member of the Church Lads Brigade or the Boys Brigade and guided to their quarters. Many a kind-hearted cavalryman lifted the youngster on to his horse, to the envy of the others. Reigate Lodge Estate, now the Orchard Road and Chartway area, accommodated the Artillery and Cavalry. A number of men were billeted in the Church Buildings and Institute in Nutley Lane and in the cottages. The troops agreed that no place previously visited had extended such a welcome as Reigate.

The following day King George V drove through Redhill to inspect the troops on the march, returning to London through Reigate.

The four photographs on these pages show the progress of the Territorials through the town. A camera has recorded the same places today.

The "Venture" coach arriving at the White Hart Hotel, Bell Street Reigate. It ran from London to Brighton via Reigate from 1908 to 1914. The White Hart stables furnished fresh horses for the next stage of the journey. A postillion on the coach would sound his horn on entering the tunnel to warn the stable hands at the hotel of their arrival. The "Venture" was owned by Alfred Vanderbilt who died as a passenger on the Lusitania when she was torpedoed in 1915.

Adam's Stores was a well-known grocers in Reigate and Redhill and occupied the premises on the corner of Tunnel Road and Church Street. They stored their wine in the vaults behind the shop. The local brewers, Mellersh & Neale also used caves in the Tunnel for storing beer. Their name can still be seen on the wall in Tunnel Road.

The London—Brighton Coach.

Wray Common Windmill, built in 1824, is a tower mill, a type developed in the 18th century. A round or octagonal tower of brick or stone was capped by the dome and sails which rotated with the wind, transmitting power to the millstone by gear wheels.

This mill ground corn for local people and was photographed in 1893, two years before falling into disuse. In 1928 the old sails were removed and replaced by dummies. The mill became a private residence in 1965.

These three L-shaped timber-framed cottages at the corner of Batts Hill and Linkfield Lane, Redhill probably date from the 16th century. Originally there may have been an open hall at the north end.

The ground floor was rebuilt using painted brick. Above, the timbering with its curved braces, was exposed and the in-filling painted. The first floor and gable end of the south wing are tile-hung, some of the casement windows having diamond shaped leaded panes.

The Reigate and Redhill Hospital Working Men's Fund annual parade,
photographed from the upper window of Dann's Studio in Brighton Road, Redhill, in 1905.

The parade, which was raising money for the Reigate and Redhill Hospital, included the Town Brass Band,
The Fire Brigades and members of the various Church organisations.

Another photograph of the Royal National Lifeboat Parade in 1907,
in Brighton Road Redhill. The lifeboat men are holding long rods with nets on the ends to collect coins
from people on the pavement. This photograph was taken from the same viewpoint but two years
after the scene on the previous page.

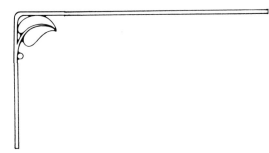

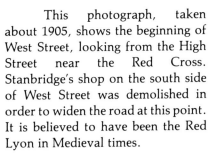

This photograph, taken about 1905, shows the beginning of West Street, looking from the High Street near the Red Cross. Stanbridge's shop on the south side of West Street was demolished in order to widen the road at this point. It is believed to have been the Red Lyon in Medieval times.

Recent alterations carried out in the surviving buildings of this group revealed some medieval timberwork which has been preserved.

The Bull's Head in Reigate High Street is an 18th century building and was originally known as the King's Head. An inn has stood on this site since 1600.

The Landlord when this photograph was taken in about 1905 was Mr. A. Crisford.

30

This was West Street Reigate in 1900, looking towards the Red Cross. Five years later the buildings on the right were demolished to enable the road to be widened.

Behind the small boy and girl a horse-drawn vehicle is coming from the direction of the High Street.

This photograph, taken about 1905, shows London Road from Park Lane. Wilson's jewellers shop stood at the end of Middle Row, which formed the island of buildings enclosed by West Street, Upper West Street and Slipshoe Street. It was demolished in 1932.

On the right of the picture is the Red Cross, unchanged today except for the rendering on the walls.

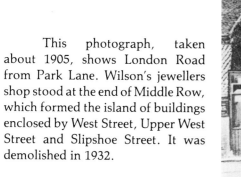

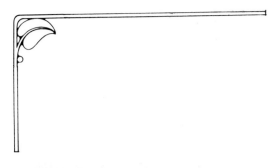

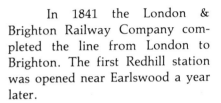

In 1841 the London & Brighton Railway Company completed the line from London to Brighton. The first Redhill station was opened near Earlswood a year later.

Only when the Ashford Branch Line was opened in 1842 was the station moved to its present site. This shows Redhill station just before the First World War.

The South Eastern and Chatham Railway branch line from Redhill to Reading was built in 1849 with a station and level-crossing on the London Road at Reigate. This 1907 photograph taken from the footbridge at Reigate station shows South Eastern region locomotive No. 187, and F-Class 4-4-0 built at the Ashford Works in 1893.

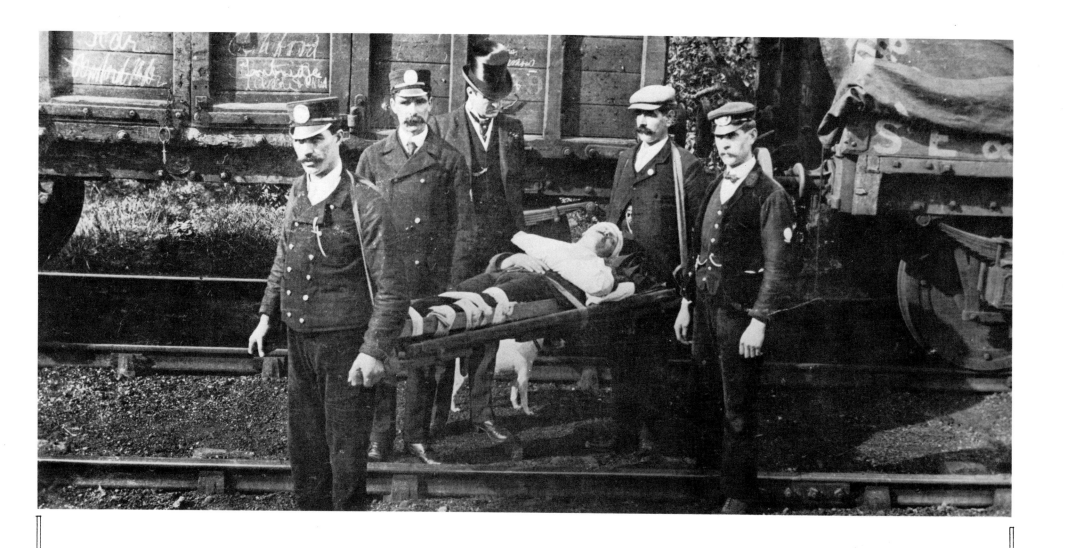

This 1908 photograph shows the Redhill No. 1. Team, winners of
the Colman Challenge Cup. No other information is available. Sir Jeremiah Colman was resident at
Gatton Park. The rolling stock is marked with the initials of the
South East & Chatham Railway.

Four "Special Events" recorded by the camera.

Top left: The Prince of Wales, later King Edward VIII, opens a new chapel and school buildings at the Southern Provincial Police Orphanage in Redhill. The date, 20th November 1923.

Top right: The event, a Pilgrim's Pageant to raise money with which to purchase Colley Hill. A group representing 'pilgrims' of the 13th and 14th centuries process from Colley Hill to the Horse Show Ground, past thousands of spectators.

Lower left: On a day in July 1913 engine trouble forced the balloon H.M.A. Delta down on Earlswood Common near Meadvale, where to the delight of residents, it remained until repairs were completed.

Lower right: Men of action, photographed in 1906. Reigate and Redhill Fire Brigades operated independently until 1909. When this picture was taken Redhill Fire Station was behind the Market Hall. The appliance was drawn by two horses.

The funeral of James Henry Laker on 19th February 1911.
Mr. Laker was a member of the Fire Brigade and was only in his thirties when he died. Here the funeral is passing
the Municipal Buildings on its way to Reigate Cemetery.

The Toll Gate and House were removed from the bottom of Reigate Hill in 1881. It stood opposite the Yew Tree which became an inn in 1841.

Reigate Hill was quarried from the 13th century and the stone used in the construction of Westminster Abbey, St. Paul's Cathedral and Hampton Court Palace.

The position of this shop, photographed before 1901 may come as a surprise. It stood at what is now the junction of Castlefield Road and Church Street. It was a white-smiths and Mr. Norris the smithy is standing in the doorway. A water stand-pipe and a gas lamp are on the grass bank in front of the smithy. The entrance in the wall at the right leads to the Reigate Lodge and its grounds.

This familiar view of Reigate as one approaches from the west has undergone subtle changes since this photograph of 1905. All the buildings still exist, but the small island and gas lamp have gone and the horse-trough now stands on the widened pavement. The cobbled gutter can still be seen in Upper West Street. This part of Reigate is a conservation area.

An East Surrey Traction Company bus turns the bend in Church Street by the gates of the Reigate Lodge Estate in 1915. A modern garage and showrooms now stand where the shops and cottages are, but the pillars at the entrance to what is now South Walk still stand. There is still a seat under the trees by the wall.

The omnibus from Reigate to Camden Town waits outside the Red Cross on a day in 1917. It is a type "B" vehicle belonging to the London General Omnibus Company. Buses of a similar type were in service as troop carriers in France at the height of the First World War.

At home, in Reigate at this time, people were queuing for bread. This photograph shows one such queue. The baker's shop is obscured by the bus.

1917. A wartime queue at the Red Cross, Reigate.

This photograph, taken during the 1914-18 War shows women bus conductors
who took the place of men serving in the Forces. The picture also shows troops dressed in "Hospital Blues", the
light-weight blue uniforms issued to men recuperating in
hospital after being wounded in action.

The single fare from Reigate to Sevenoaks was
one shilling and ninepence, about 8½p in today's coinage. The bus is a Daimler of the East Surrey Bus Company.

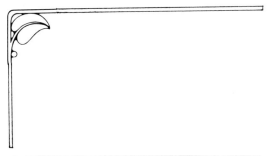

This picture shows the stalls and cattle in Redhill market. It was taken in 1903. Every Monday cattle were driven through the streets to market and the area that is now a car park resounded to the noise of pigs, sheep and cattle.

Only the upper windows of Trower's shop in this early photograph of London Road, Redhill give a clue to the scene as it is today. London Road was a quiet, tree-lined street before the 1914-18 War, with many small family shops.

Station Road Redhill again, looking west. The open top bus was run by Mr. Wickens who provided an half-hourly service from Redhill railway station to the Red Cross Hotel in Reigate.

The Wheatsheaf Hotel had been built only three years before this photograph was taken, in 1903. A policeman can be seen talking to the driver of a carriage waiting outside Gares shop.

London Road Redhill, 1904, looking south. The posters on the wall of the London Road Tea & Coffee Rooms advertise a Horse & Hound Show at Reigate and a forthcoming concert at the Market Hall.

On the right is the Queen's Arms, pulled down in 1972. The site is now occupied by offices on the corner of Queensway.

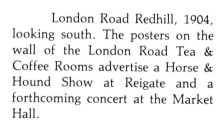

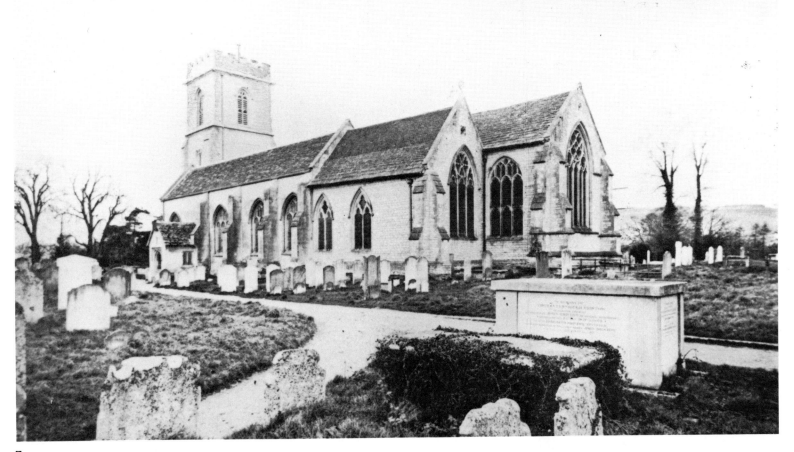

A church stood on the site of St. Marys' in the 12th century. But only after two or three hundred years did it look as it does today, becoming one of Surrey's largest Parish Churches.

During this period a new tower was built, the nave, aisle and chancel extended, the large perpendicular style windows installed and the triple screen surmounted by the Great Rood erected.

Decorations were removed during the Reformation but the rerodos was left untouched. A gallery for musicians and choir was built at the west end in the 18th century and later other galleries were added.

St. Mary's Parish Church, photographed in 1895.

In 1828 the nave roof became unsafe due to the removal of external buttresses, tie beams and king posts. Further deterioration of the roof was prevented by fitting iron tie rods and temporary buttresses.

Charles, Lord Howard of Effingham and Samuel Palmer the painter and engraver are buried here. The Church also houses the magnificent Cranston Library.

The early 18th century post mill on Reigate Heath. A mill is shown to have existed here on maps dated 1753.

From the early 19th century the Bowyer family owned the mill. It was sold in 1868 to Henry Lamson. Two years later grinding ceased. In 1880 the brick roundhouse was converted to a Chapel of Ease for St. Mary's Parish Church. Named the St. Cross Chapel, it began services that year, on September 14th. These have been held regularly ever since.

In 1906 the land freehold including the mill, cottages and Golf Club house was purchased by Reigate Heath Gold Club. The mill was then leased to the Church.

Until being purchased by Reigate Corporation in 1962, the mill had been maintained by the Golf Club. The Corporation fitted new sails, re-tarred the exterior and fitted new steps. The Council staff finished the repairs in 1964. This photograph dates from about 1895.

The Mill on the Heath.

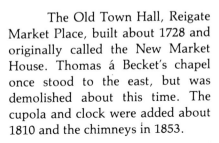

The Old Town Hall, Reigate Market Place, built about 1728 and originally called the New Market House. Thomas á Becket's chapel once stood to the east, but was demolished about this time. The cupola and clock were added about 1810 and the chimneys in 1853.

This 1914 photograph shows the Swan Hotel, which dates back to the middle of the 15th century. It was eventually replaced by shops. The Market Hotel, once the Jolly Bacchus, is on the right.

Bell Street Reigate during the first year of the Great War, looking from the Square towards the Priory. The open top bus belonged to the East Surrey Traction Company.

The west end of the Old Town Hall, Reigate, photographed in about 1908 Engraved in a window of the building is the following legend: "May we never want one of the present Royal Family to sit upon the Throne of these Kingdoms. God long preserve King George. Long live King George".

The shops on the right of the picture have remained unchanged through the years. A knife grinder with his hand-cart stands by the kerb while traffic typical of the period passes along the street.

The White Hart and The Swan were the leading hotels in Reigate for many years. The White Hart dates from the 16th century. The Prince of Wales, later, George IV often patronised the hotel on his journeys to Brighton, continuing to do so after he became king.

The hotel had extensive stables backing on to Church Street. The service road behind the present day shops was a path through the hotel gardens. The hotel was demolished in 1935. It was replaced by the present White Hart in Church Street.

Reigate Priory — A place of history.

Reigate Priory, listed as a Grade I Historic Building, was founded as an Augustinian Priory by William de Warenne in 1235. It is surrounded by public parkland.

Lord William Howard of Effingham, on being granted the Priory in 1536, converted the monastic buildings into a family residence. His son Charles, Earl of Nottingham, was educated here by John Foxe. Charles' grand-daughter Elizabeth, Countess of Peterborough, installed the magnificent Holbein fireplace.

John Parsons, wealthy brewer and later Lord Mayor of London, bought the Priory in 1681, adding the beautiful staircase, Verrio murals and imposing Eagle Gateway.

Late in the 18th century, Richard Ireland "Georgianised" the south front.

The three Earls Somers improved the building throughout the 19th century and were succeeded by Isobel who became Lady Henry Somerset of Temperance fame.

Admiral Sir David Beatty was the last private owner. In 1942 the Priory was sold to an insurance company and then bought by the Borough who, in 1945, leased it to Surrey County Council. It is now used as a school.

Photographed in about 1914 this pictures shows a Foden Steam Lorry with a cargo of barrels, outside the Black Horse. The building dates from 1760 and has been a pub since at least 1785. It was a popular meeting place after horse racing and public hangings on Reigate Heath.

Mellersh & Neale were the owners at the time of this picture. Their original brewery building still stands in Brewery Yard, Bell Street.

The Angel at Woodhatch was first used as an inn during the 18th century, when it was known as the White Horse. It stood hard by the tollgate on the turnpike road to Crawley. This picture was made soon after the toll gates were removed in 1881. The landlord then being a Mr. W. Goold.

The building dates from 1650 and was renamed The Angel in 1814.

Barber's Bakery Shop was at No. 82-84 Monson Road, Redhill. The lettering on the front of the delivery van proudly announces that it is Redhill's Steam Bakery. This was van number six and one wonders how many of these beautifully sign-written carts constituted the full fleet.

The staff of life—steam-baked and horse-drawn.

Linkfield Corner, Redhill, photographed in 1915 showing the Globe Temperance Hotel on the corner of Linkfield Lane and Station Road. There is now no surviving evidence of these buildings, the area having been cleared and laid out as a traffic roundabout and road system.

The buildings at the right and left of this old photograph have however remained virtually unchanged to this day.

The peace and normality of this photograph is in sharp contrast to the tragic events happening at this time across the English Channel. The three women in the picture may well have had husbands fighting in Gallipoli, or facing the first German poison gas attacks in France, a new and horrifying development in trench warfare in 1915.

Linkfield Corner in 1915.

The top of Park Lane as it was in 1905, looking up London Road to the school. The butcher's shop, then owned by Sydenhams, is still the same, but there have been changes to the rear elevation of the buildings on the corner of the High Street. The property to the west of London Road has also undergone considerable alteration.

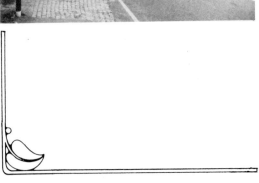

This is London Road Reigate in 1909, looking down towards Park Lane. The buildings on the right were demolished in 1932 but those on the left remain virtually unchanged. Caves beneath the road here made it unsuitable for heavy traffic and in 1924 the road collapsed under the weight of a steam-roller. Earlier, in 1860, a cave behind the Red Cross fell in causing extensive damage to five cottages.

A photograph taken in 1907 showing the corner of Alma Road and Holmesdale Road in Reigate. Some of the original building which was St. Mark's School still remains, although the headmaster's house, the building on the left, has gone. There were separate schools for boys and girls. It is strange to see St. Mark's Church with a steeple, but steeple there was, until 1918 when it was removed for reasons of safety.

Glovers Road and Lesbourne Road corner in about 1910. Strangely, the original photograph shows no lamp post on this corner, but the recent picture shows a lamp post of a style contemporary with the original.

This area was developed in about 1893 by the National Freehold Land Co., formed to enable men to purchase freehold property, thus qualifying them for parliamentary votes under the 40-Shilling franchise. Glovers Field estate was named after Ambrose Glover, one-time leaseholder of the land.

Outside the Market Hall and Assembly Rooms, Redhill, on a day in 1915.
Built on marshy land known as Rough Moors in 1860, new wings were added to the building in 1891
and 1904. The Post Office occupied the west wing from 1891 to 1932.
The building was demolished in 1982.

There were horse-chestnut trees by the Priory in the summer of 1914 and the view to the Square and Market Hotel looked very much the same as it does today. James Knight's Warehouse on the right of the photograph was later demolished and is now the entrance to the Reigate Garage.

The southern elevation of the Ancient House Bookshop didn't exist in 1914.

Bell Street Reigate, where the horse-chestnuts still flourish.

The Station Hotel at Earlswood dates from about 1878. It is now known as The Old Chestnut. The picture was taken in 1909.

The Old Chestnut.

Laker's Hotel, Redhill was originally called the Reigate Junction Hotel. It was erected soon after the opening of Redhill railway station by the M.P. for Hythe, Mr. Brockman.

In 1846 a license was granted to Richard Laker for "an inn, alehouse, and victualling house at the sign of Reigate Junction". In 1861 the name was changed to the Railway Hotel. The Laker family continued to run the hotel until about 1904.

On the death of William Laker, it was again renamed. This time, in memory of the family who had been its proprietors for nearly sixty years, it became Laker's Hotel.

Much as it was in 1904. Laker's Hotel, Redhill.

The gateway to the site of Reigate Castle photographed in 1909. It was built by
Richard Barnes in 1777 with materials from the ruins. A castle was first erected on the mound in the 11th century
by William de Warenne. After a chequered history, the castle became a ruin
by the beginning of the 18th century.

Both photographs on this page show Church Street Reigate, in 1909. Without the modern comparisons it would be difficult to locate them. The lower picture however, contains the familiar outline of the Old Town Hall.

The site of The Old Wheel Building of offices and shops was used as a maltings in the time of Charles I. Then, in 1806, a corn store and brewery. For many years before its present function, it was the Old Wheel Restaurant.

Mr. Perch ran the horse-bus service between Reigate and Redhill from 1907 until 1910.

The gardens of the Barons, the elegant Queen Anne building in Church Street are on the left of this picture. The home of Dr. Alexander Walters was the brick house on the right. These two photographs were taken in the year that Blériot first flew across the English Channel.

Lesbourne Road Reigate, in 1915. The group of self-conscious schoolboys under
the gas lamp in this war-time photograph would never have imagined that at the end of the century,
their picture would be a subject of interest and speculation.

From the present day photograph you will recognise London Road Reigate, looking towards the railway level-crossing.

The large picture, taken some eighty years earlier shows only one visual link with the present, the two buildings at the extreme right of the scene. The tree-lined gardens opposite are now the site of large office blocks.

Here is a true reflection of yesterday, of a quieter age when there was time for small courtesies and the air was not filled with the smell and sound of incessant heavy road traffic.

London Road Reigate — before the juggernauts.

Tunnel Road Reigate, an incredible engineering feat, constructed by Lord Somers in 1824. It provided a direct link between the Market Square and London Road. William Cobbett condemned it as wasteful and attracting more coaching traffic to the town.

Part of the moat above, in the Castle Grounds, was filled in and some Market Square shops were demolished. A toll-gate was installed at the entrance to the Tunnel Road and tolls charged to traffic passing through. A coach and four paid 6 pence, a coach and pair, 3 pence and for a single horse the charge was one half-penny. Pedestrians proceeded free of charge.

Ha'penny for a horse—pedestrians free.

While the Tunnel was under construction, Lord Somers' surveyor, William Constable, was cutting through the chalk of Reigate Hill, to straighten the turnpike road.

During the First World War the caves leading from the Tunnel were an ammunition store. Twenty-five years later they became air-raid shelters.

Today's view of this part of Reigate High Street looks very similar to the 1905 picture. The house with the pillars at the porch was the home of Dr. Freeman. One of W. T. Batchelor's horse-drawn carts stands at the stepped pavement. The Congregational Church, no longer existing, can be seen at the centre of the picture.

The "Vigilant" coach, on its way to Brighton, picking up passengers outside the White Hart Hotel, Bell Street, on a day in 1904.

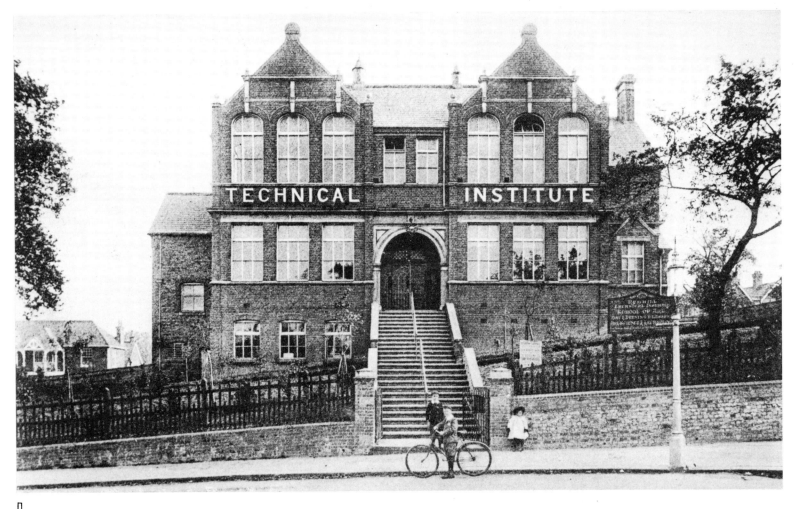

TECHNICAL INSTITUTE

"For the study of the Arts and Sciences."

"The building is erected to aid the study of the Arts and Sciences and to promote the love of learning."

When the foundation stone of the Redhill Technical Institute was laid on May 20th 1895, it carried this inscription. The Chairman of the Surrey County Council, Mr. E. J. Halsey, officiated at the ceremony. Built by J. J. Carrick, the building was designed by Baker & Penfold of Reigate.

To begin with, most classes were held in the evenings and the Institute was administered by the local Higher Education Committee of the Borough. In 1926 a principal was appointed and a junior school started.

When opened in 1895, Redhill Technical Institute was one of only four technical colleges in Surrey and over 700 students enrolled, with classes averaging 14 persons.

The buildings were enlarged over the years until the County Council purchased the nine-acre site of the old Hawthorns School at Gatton Point, where the new main building was opened in 1967.

This 1911 photograph shows the corner of the Market Hall building in Redhill Square
and the shops that were on the south side of the High Street. The sun awnings hide most of the shop names,
but Gatland Clothiers are prominent. Immediately to the left of Gatland's building,
Marketfield Road leads into Redhill Market.

 REFLECTIONS of YESTERDAY